The Story of Saga Rose & Saga Ruby

The Last Norwegian America Liners

Anders Johannessen

Contents

(Saga)

Foreword

BY ANDREW GOODSELL, SAGA GROUP EXECUTIVE CHAIRMAN

I have been lucky to sail on Saga Rose on numerous occasions over the 13 years she has been in our fleet. Each time I sail, I meet more and more people whom I have met before and, now, boarding the ship is a similar feeling to returning home after a period of absence.

In her 13 years with Saga, Rose has carried over 100,000 passengers and embarked on 11 world cruises. During her entire seafaring career she has made in excess of 40 journeys around the globe, which is more than any other ship in history.

This book is a celebration of her service and a memento to all those who have cruised with her. Saga Rose has a terrifically loyal and passionate following among our passengers, all of whom will be sad to see this lovely old lady retire. I am sure you will have your own memories to cherish of this very special ship.

Introduction

Saga Rose and Saga Ruby, the two extraordinary sister ships that make up Saga's fleet, began life as the Norwegian America Line's Sagafjord and Vistafjord. Completed in 1965 at a time when transatlantic passenger shipping was in rapid decline, the Sagafjord spent a limited amount of time on the scheduled service between Oslo and New York. Luckily she had been designed as a dual-purpose ocean liner and cruise ship from the outset and would mainly be used in the latter capacity. The Vistafjord entered service in 1973 as a full-time cruise ship. For decades the Sagafjord and Vistafjord, both of which eventually passed into Cunard Line ownership, ranked as two of the highest-rated cruise ships in the world. Their names were synonymous with luxury, voyages to exotic destinations and wealthy passengers.

Their careers eventful, Saga Rose and Saga Ruby have sailed proudly on under the Saga house flag as the last surviving Norwegian America liners. They have been kept in pristine condition and, after decades of reliable service, still offer a high-quality cruise experience. Surely the foresightedness of the Sagafjord's and Vistafjord's original designers and builders has paid off well.

Saga Rose and Saga Ruby represent a style of cruising that is all but extinct today. I was fortunate to spend a few days sailing along the Norwegian coast on Saga Rose in the summer of 2007 and have fond memories of the experience. The atmosphere on board was comfortable and relaxed, with an extremely friendly crew and excellent service. The memories I cherish the most, however, are those of the classic Saga Rose herself. I will never forget the hours spent on the observation deck underneath the bridge, overlooking the great bow, or strolling along the teak planked promenade deck at sunset. Nor will I forget the charm and elegance of the ship's wood-panelled lounges, lobbies and stairways, the grandeur of the magnificent dining room, or the reassuringly steadfast pulsation of the mighty engines as they propelled us safely across the ocean. For a young

Saga Rose in her former home port of Oslo for the final time, 20 September 2008.

Norwegian passenger ship enthusiast, the experience of sailing on the former Sagafjord was incredible.

This book pays tribute to the history of both of the Saga Ships, but it has been published specifically to commemorate the final months in service of Saga Rose, which is due to be retired by Saga in December 2009 after a highly successful career spanning 44 years. Thank you for a job well done, Saga Rose!

Oslo, July 2009
Anders Johannessen

Saga Rose as Norwegian America Line's Sagafjord. *(FotoFlite)*

From Sagafjord to Saga Rose

From the time of its formation in 1910 until 1980, the Norwegian America Line (Den Norske Amerikalinje) operated just eight passenger ships. They were the Kristianiafjord and Bergensfjord of 1913, the Stavangerfjord of 1918, the two Oslofjord's of 1938 and 1949, the Bergensfjord of 1956, the Sagafjord of 1965 and the Vistafjord of 1973. The first four NAL ships were never among the most famous or luxurious liners on the North Atlantic run to New York. The company's claim to fame, however, was the worldwide luxury cruises operated by the post-war fleet, particularly the Sagafjord and Vistafjord – both of which have survived to this day as Saga Rose and Saga Ruby and are still trading successfully as cruise ships.

NAL offered its first cruises in 1925-27 with the Stavangerfjord and Bergensfjord sailing along the Norwegian coast to the North Cape. These summer voyages were resumed in 1932, at which time NAL also began offering cruises to the Baltic, Scotland, the Faroe Islands and Iceland. In the winter of 1938-39 the Oslofjord undertook the company's first voyages from New York to the Caribbean. The first new NAL liner delivered following World War II, the second Oslofjord, was the first of the company's ships that had been designed specifically for the dual purpose of both transatlantic and cruise service. In the winter of 1951 she undertook NAL's first cruises since the inter-war years, to the Caribbean and the Mediterranean. When the second Bergensfjord was delivered in 1956, summer voyages to the Baltic and the North Cape were resumed and the number of cruises to the Caribbean and the Mediterranean were increased. Soon the ships' itineraries were expanded to include South America and the South Pacific, and in 1959 the Bergensfjord undertook NAL's first World Cruise.

In the summer of 1960, NAL's Technical Department was asked to prepare plans for another new liner. Intended as a replacement for Stavangerfjord – by then the oldest passenger ship in transatlantic service – the new vessel would primarily be employed in cruise service, her transatlantic role limited to just a handful of scheduled crossings between Oslo and New York each year. NAL's Technical Director Kaare Haug and his assistant Ditmar Kahrs were responsible for the design, as they had been for the second Oslofjord and Bergensfjord. Because the Bergensfjord had proved to be so successful, both in terms of seaworthiness and economy in operation, her design was used as the basis for the new ship. Although the hull dimensions were increased, the beam was limited by the size of Akers Mekaniske Verksted's floating drydock in Oslo, which would be used for annual overhauls.

PLACING THE ORDER

In January 1962 preliminary specifications for Norwegian America's new liner were distributed to 23 shipyards in Belgium, France, Italy and the United Kingdom. Tenders were received in March, but the final decision to build the liner was not made until July when NAL announced that negotiations with Société des Forges et Chantiers de la Méditerranée (FCM) in La Seyne-sur-Mer, France, had reached an advanced stage. The main reason why renowned shipbuilders such as the UK-based Swan, Hunter and Wigham Richardson, John Brown and Co. (Clydebank), and Fairfield Shipbuilding and Engineering Co. lost out in the bidding process was that the FCM yard was guaranteed substantial labour subsidies by the French government and, therefore, was able to quote the lowest price. In fact, these subsidies would amount to about one quarter of the NAL liner's total construction cost. The building contract for the 21,000 gross ton ship, worth 100 million Norwegian kroner (equivalent to £5 million or $24 million), was formally signed on 24 September 1962, with delivery set for 1 April 1965. In order to reduce the financial risk, the ownership of the new liner would be split 60/40 between the Norwegian America Line and the Oslo-based ship owner Leif Høegh & Co.

A team of experts had travelled on board the Bergensfjord to determine what kind of improvements could be incorporated into the design of the new NAL flagship, and in October 1962 her most important technical innovations were announced. The operation of the

The Sagafjord is launched in La Seyne-sur-Mer, France, 13 June 1964. *(Gordon Turner collection)*

The Sagafjord was given a traditional New York harbour welcome at the conclusion of her maiden voyage from Oslo, 11 October 1965 (above and opposite). *(Gordon Turner collection)*

liner would rely heavily on automation and the use of remote control, with an air conditioned, soundproofed engine control room being provided. For the first time in a transatlantic passenger liner, a bow thruster would be installed to assist in docking and undocking manoeuvres, reducing the need for tugs. Additionally, a surveillance camera covering the stern would improve the view aft from the bridge. All the features mentioned above are commonplace on board ships today, but were quite innovative back in the early 1960's. Clearly no expense would be spared in making NAL's new flagship one of the most efficient passenger liners of her time. Several rationalisation measures would be introduced in the hotel department as well, such as providing escalators for swift service between the galley and the dining room, and installing a central vacuum cleaning system throughout the passenger accommodation.

CONSTRUCTION

The first keel plates of Norwegian America's new liner were laid down at the FCM yard on 19 June 1963. Until this point the ship had been known only as yard number 1366, but a few days later it

was announced that her name would be Sagafjord. In fact, this decision had been the cause of much debate within NAL's management as the New York office had suggested it was time for the traditional "fjord" suffix to be dropped. Although this naming practice dated back to NAL's very beginning, it was argued that Americans (who made up the majority of NAL's cruising clientele) had trouble spelling and pronouncing the word, and that many did not even know what a fjord was. Norway was among several new names that were suggested, but in the end tradition prevailed. The Sagafjord was, however, a new name in the NAL fleet in its own right and, contrary to tradition, was not inspired by any geographic location.

On 13 June 1964 the Sagafjord was ready to be launched. The liner was blessed with holy water by a Catholic priest, and the French and Norwegian national anthems were played as she took to the water for the first time. In September that year it was announced that Captain Odd Aspelund had been appointed as her first Master; a company veteran of 36 years, he had been in command of the Stavangerfjord during that steamship's last transatlantic crossing from New York to Oslo in December 1963.

The Sagafjord was built on a transverse framing system, except for the double bottom and upper deck, which were longitudinally framed. The hull was of welded construction, embodying both sheer and camber in the decks. Bearing in mind the ship's occasional North Atlantic service the forebody was strengthened in excess of requirements, and the thickness of the steel used in the bottom plating, tank top and frames was also greater than required. The added weight of these measures eliminated the need for permanent ballast and lowered the centre of gravity. Additionally, 520 tons of aluminium were used in the construction of the superstructure, compensating for the hull's narrow beam and making the liner fulfil the stability requirements set by the Safety of Life at Sea 1960 convention. The Sagafjord's hull was divided into 11 watertight compartments. Designed as a two-compartment vessel, this meant she could stay afloat with any two compartments flooded.

The Sagafjord during a rough North Atlantic crossing in the late 1960's. *(NAL collection, the Norwegian Maritime Museum)*

Since the Oslofjord of 1938 Norwegian America had chosen diesel engine rather than steam turbine propulsion for their passenger ships, as the former was more economical in operation and offered improved manoeuvrability. At the time that the Sagafjord was planned there also was a lack of qualified turbine engineers in Norway, at least in NAL's view. The new liner's two Sulzer main engines, of the 9RD68 type, were built under license at FCM's engine works in Le Havre. Each had nine cylinders with a bore of 680 millimetres and a piston stroke of 1,250 millimetres. The two-stroke turbocharged engines – which were directly connected to the 61 metre long propeller shafts – each had a maximum continuous output

The Sagafjord in Cape Town. *(Ian Shiffman)*

of 12,000 brake horsepower at 150 revolutions per minute. At a service speed of 20 knots the Sagafjord would consume about 51 tons of fuel oil per day. The four-bladed propellers had a diameter of 4.8 metres and weighed 12 tons each. As mentioned above, the Sagafjord was provided with a bow thruster, a KaMeWa unit with an output of 800 horsepower. A pair of Denny-Brown AEG stabilizers, which would reduce the ship's rolling motion by up to 60 percent, was also installed. Each stabilizer fin was approximately four metres long and two metres wide. The auxiliary machinery consisted of six Bergen Diesel LSG8 type engines connected to NEBB generators of 667 kW each.

INTERIOR DESIGN AND DECORATION
The Sagafjord featured a total of 10 decks. From top to bottom these were named Bridge Deck, Sun Deck, Veranda Deck, Upper Deck, Main Deck and A, B, C, D and E Decks. The majority of public rooms could be found on Veranda Deck, one deck higher than on the Bergensfjord. Also, the Sagafjord became one of the first passenger liners in which the public rooms occupied the full width of the ship at the expense of the traditional exterior promenades that would tradition-ally have flanked them. In other words, passengers now would be able to enjoy views of the passing scenery from every public room on board except from the Saga Dining Room, which was located two decks below within the hull. The architects had originally wanted to place the dining room in the superstructure to offer diners a view of the passing scenery, but instead they opted for a more traditional but very grand solution: the Saga Dining Room had no windows but featured a two-deck high central dome and was supported by just four pillars, the result of advanced structural design.

The Sagafjord's interior design was entrusted to an international team of architects; the renowned Norwegian Frithjof S Platou and his assistant Njål R Eide served as co-ordinating designers. To ensure a degree of architectural unity throughout the ship's interiors, it was decided to use palisander wood veneers in all public rooms, lobbies and stairways. However, whole sections of the ship were divided between the various contributing architects. Platou and Eide designed the Saga Dining Room on Main Deck and the indoor swimming pool and gymnasium on C Deck, in addition to all lobbies and passenger cabins. Kay Kørbing, a Dane well known for his work on the ships of the DFDS company, was given the task of designing the Garden Lounge forward on Veranda Deck, as well as the adjoining North Cape Bar and Library located aft of this on the port and starboard sides, respectively. Kørbing also designed the forward oval-shaped staircase. In transatlantic service this portion of the ship would be reserved for the exclusive use of First Class passengers. Finn Nilsson of Oslo's Arnstein Arneberg firm (which had worked on the interiors of both the Oslofjord and the Bergensfjord) designed the Ballroom and the Veranda Café, as well as the outdoor lido area and swimming pool near the stern on Veranda Deck. Located aft on Sun Deck, and also overlooking the stern, was the dual-purpose Club Polaris. Designed by the Dutch architect Han van Tienhoven, this venue would serve as a dining room for First Class passengers in transatlantic service. Additionally, van Tienhoven designed the Gift Shop and the combined Children's Room/Dance Studio amidships on Veranda Deck. The Theatre, located close by, was designed by the Frenchman Georges Peynet.

The works of art commissioned for the Sagafjord were generally Norwegian themed. The artists represented on board were Sigurd Winge, Dagfin Werenskiold, Torstein Rittun and Carl B Gunnarson (all Norway), Phyllis Evensen (United Kingdom), van den Broek (The Netherlands) and Herman Bongard and Mandaroux (both France). Compared with previous Norwegian America liners, the Sagafjord's interior design and decoration was probably a bit more international rather than "typically Norwegian" in character, and the ship was not met with universal approval in art and design circles at home in Norway.

Bearing in mind that the Sagafjord would spend most of her time cruising rather than crossing the North Atlantic, great attention was paid to making the accommodation as comfortable as possible. The ship was fully air conditioned throughout and featured wall-to wall carpeting in all public rooms, stairways, alleyways and cabins. About 90 percent of the 275 passenger cabins were outside and all had private baths. Each cabin was equipped with a telephone, a two-channel radio and an outlet for closed-circuit television. They also

The Sagafjord in her original form, a perfect example of the streamlined Scandinavian passenger ships of the 1960's. *(Howard Onions, courtesy of Allan Ryszka-Onions)*

The Sagafjord in Southampton, October 1974. *(Howard Onions, courtesy of Allan Ryszka-Onions)*

The Story of Saga Rose and Saga Ruby

featured full-size beds rather than bunks. There were four suites on board, namely the Fridtjof Nansen and Roald Amundsen on Sun Deck and the Henrik Ibsen and Olav Trygvason on Upper Deck. Each consisted of a bedroom, living room, bath, toilet, shower and trunk room. The ship had capacity for a total of 789 passengers in transatlantic service divided between First and Tourist Class, but this would be limited to just 450 in a single class on cruises. The crew numbered 352.

TRIALS, DELIVERY AND MAIDEN VOYAGE

The Sagafjord commenced her first sea trials on 7 May 1965. By this time the outfitting of the ship had fallen behind schedule for a number of reasons, including labour difficulties, and from 1 July a penalty clause was invoked by Norwegian America Line for the delayed delivery. Because of the financial losses incurred in the building of the Sagafjord her builders had filed for insolvency, but fortunately work on the NAL flagship continued. Final sea trials took place on 4 September over the French Navy's measured mile off Toulon, during which the ship attained a maximum mean speed of 22.18 knots.

As completed the Sagafjord measured 24,002 gross tons and 13,340 net tons, with a loaded displacement of 20,160 tons and a deadweight capacity of 6,353 tons. The ship's overall length was 188.88 metres, the beam 24.38 metres and the loaded draft 8.256 metres. The masthead rose to 53.77 metres above the keel, but as the mast was of the telescopic type the top section could be lowered to 47.54 metres. Her International Maritime Organization (IMO) number was 6416043 and her call sign in the Norwegian register was L F S A. The ship was classed by Det Norske Veritas to + 1A1, ICE-C notation.

On 18 September the Sagafjord was finally handed over to Norwegian America Line, becoming the largest Norwegian passenger ship of all time and also, for a short time, the largest passenger ship in Scandinavia. The liner was named by Lucy Høegh, the wife of NAL's Chairman Leif Høegh, after which the Norwegian Mail flag and the company flag were hoisted. A luncheon was held on board before the ship left La Seyne on her delivery voyage to Oslo with about 100 invited guests. During the morning of 24 September she sailed up Oslofjord in dense fog, and while inbound in Oslo harbour the Sagafjord paused off the Aker shipyard where the Bergensfjord was dry-docked for annual maintenance work. The two liners exchanged whistle salutes and fireboats sent plumes of water into the air. The new ship then proceeded to Norwegian America's Vippetangen pier where a welcoming party including the former NAL commodore, Olaf Bjørnstad, awaited her.

The Sagafjord's first stay in her home port would be an eventful one. 139 crew members had joined the ship in La Seyne two days prior to delivery and now the remainder came aboard. At the same time all kinds of inventory and supplies had to be loaded. On 29 September the Sagafjord made an eight-hour cruise in the Oslofjord with the Norwegian monarch, King Olav V, and 400 distinguished guests. The following day the liner was open for inspection by the public, attracting 4,000 curious visitors. On 1 October a crew member fell from the boat deck and into the waters of Oslo harbour during a lifeboat drill. Luckily he escaped

from the accident without serious injuries and was able to re-board the ship following a medical examination.

The Sagafjord departed on her first transatlantic crossing, with 487 passengers, from Oslo on 2 October, calling at Kristiansand and Copenhagen en route to New York, where she arrived nine days later. The new NAL flagship was given a traditional harbour welcome with tugs and helicopters escorting her to her berth. Before she docked at Pier 45 on Manhattan's West 10th Street, an official delegation including Crown Prince Harald of Norway boarded the ship off Staten Island and sailed with her up the Hudson River. The liner spent four days in New York, during which time she was open for inspection by the public before returning to Oslo by way of Copenhagen and Kristiansand.

THE NORWEGIAN AMERICA YEARS
The Sagafjord was back in New York on 8 November 1965 to begin a series of cruises from the port. The first one, a 19-day Caribbean voyage, departed on 10 November. On the day before, the Sagafjord had been caught in the infamous Northeast Blackout. It occurred

The Sagafjord in the Kiel Canal with her telescopic mast lowered. *(Gordon Turner)*

The Sagafjord in the St. Lawrence River off Québec, September 1981. *(Marc Piché)*

in the afternoon of 9 November, affecting not just New York City, but the entire state and several neighbouring states. People were trapped inside elevators, airports had no runway lights and street traffic was in chaos. The Sagafjord, with electricity supplied by her own generators, remained tied up at her Manhattan berth with all lights ablaze, literally like a beacon in the dark night.

Power throughout New York City was not fully restored until the next morning, when the Sagafjord was due to sail. Later Life magazine published a pictorial of the blackout featuring the floodlit Sagafjord and Statue of Liberty. The title, "Graceful Lady Maintained Her Vigil over a Darkened Harbour", left it up to the individual reader to decide to which of the two ladies it referred!

On 8 January 1966 the Sagafjord left New York on her first World Cruise, a 93-day circumnavigation with 21 ports of call. The ship returned to her native Norway in May 1966 as part of a 32-day European cruise from New York, when she made her first calls in Bergen and Stavanger on Norway's west coast. This voyage was followed by a 45-day cruise, also from New York, to Northern Europe and the North Cape. Scheduled transatlantic crossings in both directions were incorporated into these voyages. In December, after another series of long cruises from New York, she returned to Oslo.

With three NAL passenger liners now in service, the Oslofjord was left to carry out most of the scheduled transatlantic crossings, with the Sagafjord and Bergensfjord being deployed mainly on cruises. By this time, however, the number of people choosing to cross the North Atlantic by sea rather than air had diminished to almost nothing, and in 1969 NAL decided there was no longer any need for the Oslofjord. She was chartered to the Costa Line in December of that year, but caught fire and sank while sailing

as Fulvia in July 1970. The Bergensfjord did not last much longer, being sold by NAL in November 1971 to the French Line which renamed her De Grasse. She was later sold to Greek interests and, under the name Rasa Sayang, burned while refitting in Piraeus in August 1980. But in December 1969 the future of Norwegian America's cruise business looked bright, and the company ordered a near-sister to the Sagafjord – to be named Vistafjord – from Swan Hunter Shipbuilders in the United Kingdom.

Like all ships, the Sagafjord would experience her share of mishaps. In one such incident, while cruising near the Svartisen glacier in Norway on 28 June 1975, the Sagafjord accidentally hit and severed a power cable strung across the Nordfjord, leaving 15 households and two local businesses without electricity for several days. The top five metres of the ship's mainmast had broken off in the impact. It was shipped to Oslo for repairs and reinstalled when she called there on 23 July. Apparently, the Sagafjord also made contact with the seabed in the Great Belt strait between the Danish islands of Zeeland and Fyn in the summer of 1977; during dry-docking at the Blohm & Voss shipyard in Hamburg later that year, a few dents in the bottom plating were discovered and had to be straightened out by using 25-30 tons of steel.

The Sagafjord's original interiors were left largely untouched for the first nine years of her service life. The first notable changes came during a regular maintenance dry-docking in Oslo from November to December 1974. The Library was turned into a Card Room with new tables replacing the writing desks, and the combined Children's Room/Dance Studio was converted to a Writing Room. The dual-purpose Club Polaris was completely redesigned by Njål R Eide, one of the ship's original interior architects. The nightclub would no longer serve as an occasional dining room for First Class passengers as Norwegian America's scheduled transatlantic service had effectively ended.

In the summer of 1974 the Sagafjord relocated to Europe after having been based mainly in New York since her introduction to the North American cruise market nine years earlier. She would offer cruises of shorter duration to the Norwegian fjords, the North Cape and Spitsbergen from departure ports such as Copenhagen, Kiel and Oslo. A year before, in May 1973, she had been joined by the new Vistafjord. The latter ship was based in New York so by moving the Sagafjord to Europe, Norwegian America was clearly trying to redistribute capacity at a time when the cruise market was in recession. Unfortunately the Sagafjord did not fare well in the European market. She returned to New York in May 1975 where she met up with the Vistafjord. Whilst there many crew members transferred between the ships, as was often the case when the two NAL liners occasionally crossed paths in ports around the world. Major crew changes were also made when the ships called at their home port of Oslo.

Norwegian America began to consider selling the Sagafjord in 1975. The operating costs of cruise ships, including crew wages and the price of fuel, had increased significantly in recent years. This made the profitability of traditional luxury liners, which carried fewer passengers than similarly sized mass-market vessels sailing in the Caribbean, particularly vulnerable. As a case in point, the Swedish American

The Sagafjord in Cape Town in the early 1980's, showing off the new deck of suites atop her superstructure. *(Ian Shiffman)*

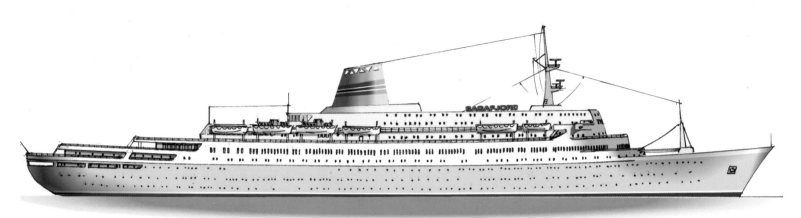

This is how the Sagafjord would have looked had she been lengthened as planned in 1979. *(Bård Kolltveit)*

Line withdrew from the cruise business in 1975 and the Gripsholm and Kungsholm – which had been considered to be the Sagafjord and Vistafjord's greatest rivals in the luxury market – were sold. There were rumours that the Greek Karageorgis Lines, which had purchased the Gripsholm, was interested in the Sagafjord for Mediterranean cruise service. In any case, serious negotiations between Norwegian America and the Deutsche Atlantik Linie for a charter of the ship actually did take place. Plans were underway to rename the liner Hanseatic, repaint her with a white hull and red funnel with a white star (the Deutsche Atlantik livery and logo), and register her in Bermuda to reduce costs. However, the deal failed to materialize and the Sagafjord sailed on, though still under a cloud of uncertainty.

Following the completion of a Mediterranean cruise in New York on 15 October 1976, the Sagafjord was laid up at the Norfolk Shipbuilding and Drydock

Company in Virginia to await a final decision regarding her future. Just 25 crew members remained on board for watch-keeping and maintenance duties, while many of their colleagues transferred to the Vistafjord. However, after much consideration, Norwegian America decided to keep the Sagafjord. Before the ship returned to service in April 1977, 25 of the single-berth cabins on board were made into doubles. This increased the passenger capacity to 480, improving the ship's revenue earning potential.

In 1979 detailed plans were worked out for a potential lengthening of the Sagafjord. By inserting a new 28-metre section just forward of the ship's funnel the passenger capacity could be further increased, to 750, by adding 246 berths. On Veranda Deck there would be room for a new bar and a casino, while below decks new auxiliary engines and generators, new evaporators and a sewage treatment plant would be added. It was estimated that it would take 16 weeks and cost 125 million Norwegian kroner to complete this work. Tenders had been invited from a small group of shipyards, but the final decision would depend on the development in the cruise market, according to NAL.

Instead, in December 1979, it was announced that the Norwegian America Line intended to merge its passenger division with Royal Viking Line, another Norwegian-owned luxury cruise operator. Ownership of the new company would be split equally between NAL/Leif Høegh & Co, Det Bergenske Dampskibsselskab and Det Nordenfjeldske Dampskibsselskab. It is likely that the Sagafjord and Vistafjord would have been repainted with white hulls and renamed Royal Viking Saga and Royal Viking Vista, joining the existing fleet, comprising the Royal Viking Star, Royal Viking Sky and Royal Viking Sea. The board of directors at Bergenske, however, felt that the Sagafjord was too old for the Royal Viking fleet and should be sold. NAL and Leif Høegh found this unacceptable and the merger plans were called off. Instead, in May 1980 a new joint venture company was formed under the name of Norwegian America Cruises (NAC), effectively separating NAL's passenger and cargo divisions. NAL and Leif Høegh & Co each had a

50 percent stake, Høegh paying 30 million Norwegian kroner (equivalent to $6 million) for its increased ownership in the Sagafjord and Vistafjord. However, by the end of the year NAL had sold its remaining shares in Norwegian America Cruises to Høegh for about 150 million Norwegian kroner (equivalent to $30 million).

NAC opted for a vertical rather than longitudinal expansion of the Sagafjord, as plans had also been prepared for adding a new deck of suites atop the ship's bridge. The Blohm & Voss yard in Hamburg was awarded the 60 million kroner contract (equivalent to $12 million) in competition with CMR Marseille, France. The rebuilding work was undertaken from 25 October until 18 December 1980. The Sagafjord's beautiful exterior was undeniably compromised, although her new profile almost resembled that of the Vistafjord (which had always been one deck higher) when viewed from a distance. The ship's gross tonnage increased to 24,109, the net tonnage to 13,820 and the displacement to 20,270 tons. Named Terraced Sun Deck, the new top deck structure housed 15 suites. The two largest ones were named Saga and Vista respectively, each having

a separate living room and bedroom with views over the bow. The 13 penthouse suites further aft all had a private balcony, but the Saga and Vista suites actually lacked this and so a private balcony was incorporated aft of the new superstructure section for use by their occupants. As a result of this work, the Sagafjord gained an additional 32 berths, bringing the total passenger capacity to 509 and the number of cabins to 294.

Njål R Eide, who was in charge of the design work during the refit, was given the task of refurbishing the Sagafjord's public rooms and cabins in a more modern style. The Ballroom was extensively remodelled, receiving new fabrics, furniture and wall coverings. New furniture was also added in the Saga Dining Room, the Garden Lounge and the North Cape Bar. The Writing Room was made into a Casino and an outdoor bar was built on the pool deck. At the same time many technical upgrades were carried out behind the scenes. Most importantly, the original auxiliary machinery was replaced by six new Bergen Diesel LDG6 type engines of 670 kW each. A new air conditioning system and new evaporators were installed as well. The bridge was

The Sagafjord in Cunard Line colours. *(Ian Shiffman)*

The Gripsholm aground in the Öresund strait on 5 August 1996 (above). The ship sustained damage to one of her propellers and went to the Lloyd Werft yard in Bremerhaven for repairs (below).

(Photo above: Ralf Baumanns, below: Axel Menzer)

equipped with new radars and the four cruise tenders were overhauled, three of them receiving new engines.

During most of her career the Sagafjord had remained based in New York, offering long cruises to destinations such as Northern Europe, the Baltic and Scandinavia, the Mediterranean and the Pacific Ocean. Most years she had also carried out a three-month World Cruise. Occasionally, though, the ship had been based in Port Everglades, Florida, for Caribbean voyages, and in 1978 and 1980 spent several months cruising in the Mediterranean out of Genoa, Italy. In the summer of 1981, however, NAC based the Sagafjord in San Francisco for a series of cruises to Alaska. For the first time, cruises from New York to New England and Canada would also be offered. The Sagafjord would be deployed on these itineraries for many years to come, spending most of her time in North American waters, but still doing a World Cruise or extended voyage each year. Her younger sister, the Vistafjord, on the other hand, would spend an increasing amount of her time in Europe.

THE CUNARD YEARS

In May 1983 it was announced that the Sagafjord and Vistafjord had been sold to the legendary Cunard Line, a subsidiary of the UK-based Trafalgar House Investments. In October, following the completion of the £47 million (equivalent to $73 million) takeover, the former Norwegian America liners were delivered to their new owner. Thus an important chapter in Norwegian passenger shipping history, dating back to 1910, had come to an end. It is interesting to note that both ships retained their original names, and that they would be marketed under the brand name of Cunard-NAC for the remainder of the decade. This reflects how well known and respected the two Norwegian liners were in the luxury cruise market.

Although the Sagafjord and Vistafjord retained their grey hull colour, their buff funnels were repainted in Cunard's traditional red and black funnel colours. (As the story goes, it was the new look of the Norwegian America sisters that prompted Cunard to repaint the flagship Queen Elizabeth 2 in a similar livery in 1982.

It did not look particularly good on the QE2, however, and she was repainted with a black hull the following year.) The registry was changed to the Bahamas (the Sagafjord's new call sign was C 6 Z U), but the ships largely retained their Norwegian deck and engine crews and Scandinavian/European service staff.

Immediately after having been taken over by Cunard, the Sagafjord was dry-docked at Todd Shipyards in San Francisco from October until December 1983. The main objective of the $10 million refit was to increase the ship's passenger capacity, bringing her more in line with the Vistafjord. The superstructure aft of the funnel was expanded with a new deck level, named Terraced Officers Deck, being created. This section housed 11 penthouse balcony suites, ten of which could be combined to form double penthouses. On Promenade Deck (formerly known as Sun Deck) 15 new deluxe cabins were built in place of Club Polaris. Additionally, 12 new passenger cabins were built in former crew areas forward on Main Deck, while five passenger cabins fully aft on

A Deck were replaced by new crew accommodation. A two-year refurbishment of all cabins on board was initiated, which entailed the replacement of the darker, traditional colours with lighter decor.

During the refit changes were made in the public areas as well. First and foremost a new Club Polaris, spanning two decks and featuring floor-to-ceiling windows overlooking the stern, was built in place of the former outdoor sports area aft on Promenade Deck. In order to accommodate the increased passenger load, the Saga Dining Room was extended forward at the expense of five passenger cabins. At the same time window openings were cut in the sides of the hull (17 on the port side and 23 on the starboard), admitting natural daylight into the space and offering diners sea views for the first time. The Casino was enlarged to incorporate a new Photo Shop, and a Health Spa was created by the indoor swimming pool. Cunard entrusted the spa operation to the renowned Golden Door, the same company that was responsible for the spa on the QE2. Following the refit, the Sagafjord was re-measured at 24,474 gross tons and 9,091 net tons, while the loaded displacement increased to 20,552 tons and the deadweight capacity decreased to 4,089 tons. The passenger capacity increased to 589 and the number of cabins to 322.

With all the improvements in place, the Sagafjord was poised for a decade of successful cruise service with Cunard. The company would continue to spend a great deal of money on keeping the ageing lady shipshape. This included not just cosmetic touch-ups, but technical upgrades as well. During dry-docking in Rio de Janeiro, Brazil, from November until December 1985, the Sagafjord received a new pair of Stone Manganese four-bladed propellers designed to offer better fuel economy and reduce vibration. Each had a diameter of 4.9 metres and weighed 9.4 tons. At the same time the air conditioning plant was modernised and a new chiller, which would increase capacity, was added. Two years later, while at Northwest Marine Iron Works in Portland, Oregon in December 1987, the galley received new equipment and various alterations were made to comply with United States Public Health requirements. Later still, at the Newport News Shipbuilding yard in Virginia in December

The Gripsholm in Southampton, October 1996. *(John Adams)*

Saga Rose in Dover on her inaugural cruise, May 1997. *(Saga)*

1993, the Saga Dining Room and the Ballroom were extensively refurbished. This work was carried out by the renowned Tillberg Design firm of Sweden.

On 12 June 1995, while on her way to Alaska, the Sagafjord suffered engine problems and arrived in Vancouver two days behind schedule. Here the 461 passengers disembarked and the following cruise was cancelled in order for repairs to be made. In December that year Cunard announced that the Sagafjord would be withdrawn from service on 22 September 1996. This was not because of the recent technical problems – the ship simply was no longer considered profitable enough. Cunard had, in fact, been trying to sell the Sagafjord for the past five years.

In April 1996 Trafalgar House and its subsidiaries were acquired by the Kværner conglomerate, meaning that the Sagafjord and Vistafjord returned to Norwegian ownership for a short while. Kværner was not particularly interested in the Cunard Line, however, and within two years the cruise line was sold to the Miami-based Carnival Corporation, the world's largest operator of cruise ships.

On the morning of 26 February 1996, during her final World Cruise for Cunard, the Sagafjord experienced a serious fire in her auxiliary engine room which resulted in a complete blackout on board. The ship had been on her way from Hong Kong to Kota Kinabalu, Malaysia, but was left without power in the South China Sea some 230 miles west of Manila. After about three hours the fire appeared to be out, but because of the extreme heat in the affected engine room area it self-ignited and started burning again. Another two hours later, with very little water left for extinguishing the fire, the situation was finally brought under control. However, there was no power, lights, air conditioning or running water on board, making the situation quite uncomfortable for both passengers and crew. Tugs were called in to tow the Sagafjord to Subic Bay in the Philippines, where she arrived in the early hours of 1 March. Here the 492 passengers disembarked, being transferred to Cunard's Queen Elizabeth 2 and Royal Viking Sun, both of which were also on World Cruises at the time. Having completed preliminary repairs, the Sagafjord set her course for Singapore where she was to go into drydock at the Sembawang Shipyard. On 15 April, however, she responded to distress calls coming from the Harran, a Turkish freighter which had developed a leak during bad weather and was sinking near the Spratly Islands west of the Philippines. The 26 crew members, hailing from Turkey, Russia and Bulgaria, had gone into the lifeboats by the time the Sagafjord arrived on the scene and took them on board. Apart from one man having suffered a broken leg, they were all in good shape.

Saga Rose on her first visit to Antarctica during the 2004 World Cruise. *(Saga)*

TRANSOCEAN INTERLUDE

With the damage to her engine room fully repaired, the Sagafjord left Singapore in June. By this time she was no longer officially part of the Cunard fleet; following the engine room fire the company had cancelled the ship's remaining sailings and chartered her to Transocean Tours, a German cruise operator, for nine months. Transocean had originally chartered another vessel, the Regent Sea (the former Gripsholm of the Swedish American Line), but this deal fell through at the last minute. Transocean had already heavily promoted their new ship as the Gripsholm so there was no turning back now – and that is how the Sagafjord came to assume the name of her once great rival.

The Gripsholm arrived in Bremerhaven, Germany, on 12 July 1996 sporting a white funnel with a blue top and the Transocean logo in place. This was the first time the Bremen-based company had its logo displayed on a chartered cruise ship. A formal renaming ceremony took place at the Columbuskaje on 16 July, with the popular singer Caterina Valente serving as godmother. The Gripsholm set sail on her first voyage for Transocean later that afternoon, still manned mainly by Norwegian officers. The Transocean charter would see the ship continue worldwide cruising. In the summer of 1996 the former Sagafjord returned to Norwegian waters for the first time in 16 years, and in the winter of 1997 she undertook a 40-day cruise from Hamburg across the Atlantic to the eastern coast of Canada and the United States. During her time under charter to Transocean, the Gripsholm also visited such ports as Rio de Janeiro, Brazil, and ventured into the Mediterranean.

At the very beginning of the Transocean charter, however, the Gripsholm had suffered an embarrassing accident. In the evening of 4 August 1996, while sailing at 18 knots through Öresund (the strait separating Denmark and Sweden), the ship firmly grounded herself on a sandbank in just five metres of water. As it later turned out, she had been 300-400 metres outside of the shipping lane and two of her officers were later suspended from duty. The next day the 601 passengers, mainly of German and Ukrainian nationality, were taken ashore to the Swedish town of Landskrona by the ship's own lifeboats and returned in buses to Copenhagen and Kiel. Three days later five tugs managed to free the Gripsholm from the sandbank and she proceeded to a nearby Helsingborg shipyard for inspection, where it was revealed that one of the propellers had been damaged in the grounding. The ship then went to the Lloyd Werft yard in Bremerhaven for repairs, returning to service on 18 August.

THE SAGA YEARS

Saga Holidays had been marketing berths on cruise ships sailing out of the United Kingdom for many years and, frustrated by its dependence upon other cruise lines, decided it was time to acquire a vessel of its own in order to offer cruises 'tailor-made' for its passengers. The former Sagafjord was deemed to be very suitable because she had the long cruising range Saga required as well as spacious cabins, a good proportion of which were single-berth. Specialising in providing services for people over the age of 50 – ranging from holidays to financial products – Saga

was founded in 1951. Although Transocean Tours had expressed an interest in buying the Gripsholm, the price being asked by Cunard was too high. Instead in October 1996, the ship was sold to the UK-based Saga Group and renamed Saga Rose.

The Gripsholm arrived in Southampton in April 1997 where she went into A&P's King George V drydock. Here she was transformed into Saga Rose, being repainted with a dark blue hull and a deep yellow funnel with a blue and white top. Some technical work was done and several of the public rooms were extensively refurbished by Alison Clixby of SMC Design to better suit the tastes of Saga's almost exclusively British clientele. Her new more luxurious interior and classic style was wholly in keeping with the classic cruising that Saga had in mind for her.

On 16 May the ship was formally renamed Saga Rose during a ceremony in Dover. Four days later, after a three-day shakedown cruise, she set sail on her first Saga voyage with fare-paying passengers bound for the Western Mediterranean. British officers

Saga Rose inbound to Oslo, July 2007. *(Anders Johannessen)*

Saga Rose makes an impressive sight at speed. *(Saga)*

The Story of Saga Rose and Saga Ruby

were in command, the remainder of the crew being multinational. Saga Rose's first year of service was challenging, but she soon settled down to become, once again, a ship of great and increasing popularity. Saga Rose continued to roam the world, cruising from British ports such as Dover and Southampton to even the most remote destinations, ranging from Spitsbergen to the Pacific to the Far East.

In October 1997 Saga Rose returned to A&P Southampton for further technical work. This was the second part of the £15 million refit Saga had planned for the ship, intended to bring her in line with the new SOLAS 1997 fire safety requirements. Her first World Cruise departed on 7 January 1998.

Since her first World Cruise with NAL in 1966, Saga Rose is believed to have completed more circumnavigations than any other passenger ship in existence. During the 2004 World Cruise Saga Rose made her historic first visit to Antarctica. On 26 January she called into the Falkland Islands before heading down to the Antarctic Peninsula. Her delighted passengers used the Polarcirkel boats to land on Half Moon Island, Waterboat Point and to sail into the Caldera that is Deception Island. While there, the thermally heated water from the lava beach gave passengers the remarkable opportunity to go swimming.

In December 2006 several of Saga Rose's public rooms were extensively refurbished while in drydock at the Blohm + Voss shipyard in Hamburg. This task was entrusted to Clixby Associates, the design firm set up by Alison Clixby together with her husband. Notably, the Britannia Lounge and North Cape Bar were refurbished in a brighter colour scheme, the Lido Café was rebuilt with an improved buffet section, and the Dining Room received a trio of striking new chandeliers. That the 41-year old Saga Rose was treated to a £4 million facelift at such a late stage in her career serves to demonstrate the commitment made by Saga to keep the classic ship in pristine condition. Since purchasing Saga Rose in 1997 the company has spent a substantial amount of money both in front of and behind the scenes, from modernising the bathrooms in passenger cabins to returning the ship's veteran engines back to good health. Saga Rose now looks better than ever and, despite the many refurbishments carried out over the years, the original character of the interiors has not been compromised. Public rooms, lobbies and stairways are still adorned with elegant wood panelling, and many of the original architectural details remain intact. Although many of the artworks from the time of the Sagafjord have long since been removed, the few that remain have been preserved under Saga ownership.

20 May 2007 marked the 10th anniversary of the former Sagafjord's time in service as Saga Rose. Incidentally the ship called in the French port of Toulon that day, close to the site where she had been built 42 years earlier. The celebrations included a formal reception for civic and local port dignitaries, a cocktail party and a special French-themed dinner. Representatives of the port authorities were given a glass plaque by Captain Neil Broomhall which read: "Presented to the people of Toulon, the birthplace of Saga Rose on the tenth anniversary of the formation of Saga Shipping Company Ltd."

2007 also saw the introduction of the first ever Mystery Cruise. Passengers joined Captain Alistair McLundie on a voyage where they would only know each destination as they arrived into port. Surprisingly, perhaps, this cruise sold out in a matter of weeks.

On 5 January 2008 Saga Rose set sail on another World Cruise from Southampton. On the fifth day of the voyage, as she left Funchal, the ship completed one million miles of cruising under Saga's ownership.

The times are catching up with Saga Rose. The new SOLAS fire safety requirements which come into force on 1 October 2010 dictate, among other things, that all passenger ships must be constructed of incombustible materials. This means that the fine woodwork that provides so much of the charm of Saga Rose's interiors is one of the main reasons why she is unable to continue in service. This is ironic as the ship, with its recently installed fire alarms and high fog sprinkler systems, has never been safer.

The former Norwegian America liners together at Southampton on 5 January 2009, as Saga Rose was due to commence her final World Cruise and Saga Ruby about to set off on her African Odyssey cruise. *(Andrew Sassoli-Walker)*

It was originally planned that Saga Rose would be retired in September 2010, but in October 2008 Saga announced that the ship would be withdrawn from service the following year. Her final voyage, a 37-day cruise of the Mediterranean, will depart from Southampton on 30 October 2009. Bringing the ship's career with Saga full circle, Captain David Warden-Owen will be in command, just as he was on the first voyage in May 1997. On board there will be a special programme of activities and entertainment, and a farewell party.

So, what does the future hold for Saga Rose beyond 2009? She is in very good condition for a ship of her age and has been continually updated by Saga. Former ocean liners have ended up in various different resting places. The famous Queen Mary, Queen Elizabeth 2 and Rotterdam have all found futures as hotel ships and conference centres in ports from Long Beach in California to Dubai. A number of famous liners have been lost to ship-breakers or the perils of the sea, whilst others remain laid up at quiet anchorages awaiting a decision as to their fate. Saga Rose clearly has the potential to continue welcoming holiday-makers on board for many years to come, if a suitable resting place can be found. Whatever the future holds for this classic ship, she will be fondly remembered by all those who have sailed on her.

Saga Rose in Pictures

All photos: Anders Johannessen

Stairs

Dining room

Lounges

Lounges

Decks

Decks

Original artworks

Cabin

SAGAFJORD OSLO

Bridge

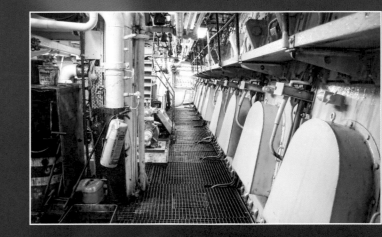

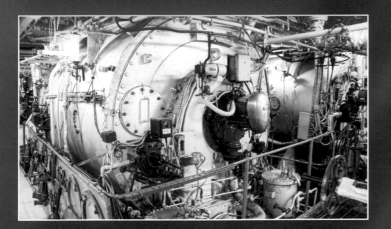

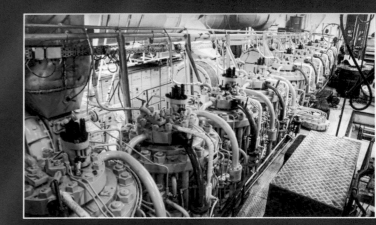

Engine room

From Vistafjord to Saga Ruby

In November 1969, after much consideration, the Norwegian America Line decided to go ahead with its plans for a new cruise ship. On 5 December a building contract was signed with Swan Hunter Shipbuilders in Wallsend on Tyne near Newcastle, the same yard that had delivered the Bergensfjord in 1956. It called for the construction of a 25,000-gross ton ship to be delivered by September 1973. Again, the financing of the new liner would be split 60/40 between NAL and Leif Høegh & Co. Unlike the Sagafjord, however, she was not ordered at a fixed price and the construction cost eventually reached a staggering 297 million kroner (equivalent to £19.2 million or $35 million).

CONSTRUCTION

In January 1970 Swan Hunter allocated the building of Norwegian America's new vessel, known as yard number 39, to the Neptune yard at Wallsend on Tyne. The keel laying took place on 19 April 1971, but another ten months passed before the ship's name was announced. She would become the third Vistafjord in the company's history, inheriting the name from a NAL cargo liner which would be renamed Kongsfjord. Incidentally, the latter vessel too had been built by Swan Hunter, in 1960.

Like her post-war predecessors, the Vistafjord was designed by Kaare Haug and his assistants in NAL's Technical Department. Her design was largely based on Sagafjord and it is interesting to note that no model tests were carried out for the new ship. The naval architects decided against the inclusion of a bulbous bow despite the potential half-a-knot gain in speed. They were worried that it might affect the new liner's sea-keeping qualities compared to the excellent performance of the Sagafjord. However, bulbous bows had become the norm in passenger ship design by the early 1970's and, seen in retrospect, NAL's architects were very conservative. Basically, the Vistafjord's hull form had originated with the Oslofjord of 1949. Almost

Saga Ruby as Norwegian America Line's Vistafjord. *(FotoFlite)*

uniquely among the cruise ships of her time, the Vistafjord was built with sheer and camber in the decks in the manner of traditional shipbuilding. She was also given very fine hull lines with a block coefficient of just 0.57 – slightly less than her older sister's 0.58.

The Vistafjord would also feature the traditional, pyramid-shaped profile which characterized the post-war Norwegian America liners. The long bow was followed by a stepped back bridge front, and the funnel was centrally placed atop the superstructure, which receded aft in terraced decks towards the stern. For all the reasons stated above, the Vistafjord today is considered by many to be the last "classic" passenger liner ever built. In terms of exterior styling, on the other hand, she clearly represented a more modern version of the streamlined Sagafjord. The bridge front in particular had a more angular look to it, as did the taller funnel, reflecting the design trends of the 1970's.

The Vistafjord's machinery was largely similar to that of the eight year older Sagafjord, her Sulzer main engines again being of the 9RD68 type. By then a rather dated model, this engine was chosen by NAL because of its proven reliability. The Vistafjord's units were built by George Clarke & N.E.M. Each featured nine cylinders with a bore of 680 millimetres and a piston stroke of 1,250 millimetres, and had a maximum output of 12,000 brake horsepower each at 150 revolutions per minute. At a service speed of 20 knots, with each engine working at an economic loading of 5000 kW at 135 rpm, the Vistafjord would consume about 48 tons of fuel oil per day. The four-bladed propellers each had a diameter of 4.8 metres and a weight of 12 tons. The auxiliary machinery consisted of six Bergen Diesel RSGB8 type engines connected to NEBB generators of 690 kW each. She was given a slightly more powerful, 1,000-horsepower KaMeWa bow thruster than the Sagafjord, but was equipped with a similar pair of Denny-Brown AEG stabilizers.

The Vistafjord was launched on 15 May 1972. Construction progressed at a rapid pace and by August that year areas such as the indoor swimming pool and gymnasium on C Deck were completely finished. The construction schedule benefited from good advance planning and the limited use of sub-contracting. The pre-fabrication of cabins, among other things, also speeded up the building process.

More than 1,300 shipyard workers were employed in the construction of Vistafjord. In March 1973 a group of 700 outfitters went on strike, threatening to delay the delivery of the ship because they had not received their fair share of a £23,000 bonus awarded to about 500 carpenters by Norwegian America for the speedy completion of the interior outfitting. (In fact the delivery date had been moved forward by a whole four months.) The matter was resolved after NAL paid a £50,000 bonus.

INTERIOR DESIGN AND DECORATION
The Vistafjord's general arrangement was largely identical to that of the Sagafjord. The main difference between the two ships was that new ship's superstructure was one deck taller. Also, the Vista Dining Room

The Vistafjord on trials in the North Sea, 7 April 1973. *(Swan Hunter Shipbuilders, author's collection)*

The Vistafjord in Oslo on her maiden voyage, May 1973. *(Bård Kolltveit)*

was located one deck higher, on Upper Deck, just below the public rooms on Veranda Deck. Compared to the Sagafjord's impressive domed dining room it was just a single deck in height, but instead featured sea views through large windows on either side. This had become a trend in cruise ship design by the early 1970's.

With the exception of Georges Peynet, the same team of international architects that had been responsible for the Sagafjord's interiors was retained for the Vistafjord. Once again the renowned Frithjof S Platou served as co-ordinating designer, while Njål R Eide was given a greater degree of responsibility this time around. Eide designed the Vista Dining Room and Club Viking, as well as the indoor swimming pool on C Deck, the shops, and the amidships and aft staircases and lobbies. Kay Kørbing of Copenhagen once again was responsible for the public rooms forward on Veranda Deck, namely the Garden Lounge, North Cape Bar, Library and Writing Room, Norse Lounge and Club 52, as well as the forward stairway and lobbies. Finn Nilson of the Oslo-based Arnstein Arneberg architectural firm, meanwhile, designed the Ballroom, Lido Café and

outdoor swimming pool aft on Veranda Deck, in addition to all the passenger cabins and suites. Curiously, none other than Kaare Haug, the Vistafjord's chief naval architect, designed the interiors for the Theatre.

Several major artworks were commissioned from Scandinavian artists to decorate the public rooms. In the main hall on Veranda Deck there was a large tapestry woven by Anne Lise Knudtzon, while the North Cape Bar was adorned with clay sculptures by Lise Honore. Carl B. Gunnarson contributed a massive wrought iron and brass decoration found in Club Viking, and a large painting by Tove Krafft was hung in the main staircase between Promenade Deck and Veranda Deck. The Vista Dining Room contained several lithographs by Suzanne Øgaard and two large brass and enamel decorations by Jørleif Uthaug.

Since the construction of the Sagafjord in the early 1960's the subject of fire safety on passenger ships had been given much attention. Consequently the Vistafjord's interiors were made up of incombustible materials in accordance with the latest requirements.

This did not prevent public rooms, lobbies and stairways from being decorated with one millimetre thick wood veneers, for which padauk, a richly grained hardwood from Thailand, was used. Hence the Vistafjord's interiors would have the same luxurious, warm feel as those of the Sagafjord, though the overall effect was decidedly lighter and the colours brighter.

On average the Vistafjord's passenger cabins were somewhat smaller than those of the Sagafjord and, consequently, did not offer as much space for storing luggage. However, about 80 percent of the cabins were outside. Compared to the Sagafjord the bathrooms were equipped with showers rather than baths, taking up less space and increasing the number of berths on board. Up on Sun Deck there were several deluxe single cabins which could be combined to form suites with a shared sitting room. They were named Atlantic, Pacific, Caribbean, Baltic, Mediterranean and Arctic, respectively, while the four largest suites on board – each featuring twin bedrooms and a separate sitting room – were named King Olav, King Harald, King Haakon and King Magnus. As completed the

Vistafjord had capacity for 500 passengers in regular cruise service, though a total of 635 berths could be found in the 343 cabins. The crew numbered 390.

TRIALS, DELIVERY AND MAIDEN VOYAGE
The Vistafjord left the Neptune yard for three days of sea trials on 6 April 1973, and although she encountered a strong gale in the North Sea, she easily attained her required 20-knot service speed. Although she had the same propulsion power as the Sagafjord, the Vistafjord proved slightly faster as her maximum speed exceeded 22.5 knots.

As completed the Vistafjord measured 24,292 gross tons and 12,770 net tons, with a loaded displacement of 20,167 tons and a deadweight capacity of 5,954 tons. The ship's overall length was 191.08 metres, the beam 24.38 metres and the loaded draft 8.526 metres. The masthead rose 52.77 metres above the keel, but as the mast was of the telescopic type the top section could be lowered to pass under bridges. The Vistafjord's International Maritime Organization (IMO) number was 7214715 and her call sign in the

The Vistafjord in Cape Town (above and next page). *(Ian Shiffman)*

(Ian Shiffman)

Norwegian register was L F V I. The ship was classed by Det Norske Veritas to + 1A1, ICE-C notation.

During the final week at the Neptune yard the Vistafjord was visited by 12,000 people, many of whom were the families of yard workers who wanted to see for themselves what had been accomplished. The ship was handed over to Norwegian America Line on 15 May 1973, exactly one year after her launch. Prior to leaving the builder's yard the Vistafjord was formally named by Agnes Cecilie Henriksen, the wife of NAL's Managing Director Hans Christian Henriksen, and once the ship had cleared the Tyne the flag changing ceremony took place. The Vistafjord then set sail across the North Sea to Norway with about 200 invited guests, and they were joined the next day in Stavanger by another 125 passengers for the last leg of the delivery voyage to Oslo. The Vistafjord docked at NAL's Vippetangen pier in the afternoon of 17 May, at the height of the Norwegian Independence Day celebrations. It could hardly have been a more fitting occasion for the maiden arrival of the last Norwegian America liner.

By this time, however, Norwegian America's passenger ship fleet consisted of just the Vistafjord and Sagafjord. The company's first post-war transatlantic liner, the Oslofjord, had been chartered to the Costa Line in 1969, but caught fire and sank while sailing for the Italians as the Fulvia during the following year. In 1971 the Bergensfjord too had left the NAL fleet, having been sold to the French Line. Together with the insurance sum received for the loss of the Oslofjord, this put Norwegian America Line in a good financial position when taking delivery of the new $35-million Vistafjord.

During the Vistafjord's first stay in Oslo, King Olav V requested a visit to the ship. On 22 May he was given a guided tour by Captain Roald Halvorsen, who had transferred from the Sagafjord to take command of the company's new flagship. Later that day the Vistafjord departed on her maiden voyage to New York, calling at Kristiansand and Copenhagen en route. She arrived at her destination on 31 May with just 215 passengers on board, proof that the era of transatlantic passenger shipping was indeed a thing of the past. However, the Vistafjord had been built exclusively for cruising, her North Atlantic crossings being merely repositioning voyages. In fact, Norwegian America Line had stopped keeping separate passenger statistics for the transatlantic crossings the year before.

The Vistafjord departed from New York on 1 June on a "cruise to nowhere" for the benefit of the American Cancer Society. On board were about 600 distinguished passengers, including New York Governor Nelson Rockefeller and the Norwegian Ambassador to the United States. The six-hour fundraiser voyage brought in $200,000.

THE NORWEGIAN AMERICA YEARS

Having been introduced to the media and travel trade, the Vistafjord departed from New York on her first cruise - a four-day voyage to Bermuda – on 7 June 1973. The remainder of the year would see the ship undertake more far-ranging voyages in the traditional Norwegian America manner, some of more than 40 or 50 days' duration and visiting Northern Europe, the Baltic and Scandinavia, the Mediterranean and South America, respectively. The ship's first World Cruise began in New York on 4 January 1974; a circumnavigation that lasted 94 days and visited 23 different ports.

In the summer of 1975 the Vistafjord was relocated from New York to Europe, offering cruises from departure ports such as Southampton, Tilbury and Hamburg. She spent the following winter sailing in the Caribbean out of Port Everglades, Florida, before returning to Europe. With some exceptions this would be the ship's annual pattern of deployment for years to come.

The Vistafjord would experience her share of incidents as she sailed the world. During the early hours of 26 August 1974 a tour guide went missing while the ship was underway from Gdynia, Poland, to Copenhagen, Denmark. A big rescue operation was launched and several ships aided the Vistafjord's crew in the search for the man, but he was never found. Later, on 11 March 1975 while bound for Istanbul, the ship came to the aid of a sailor who had fallen ill on a Turkish vessel. He was taken on board and treated in the hospital. While cruising in Spitsbergen on 11 July the same year, one of the Vistafjord's waiters went missing. He was believed to have fallen overboard and drowned or frozen to death in the icy Arctic waters.

In December 1975 the Vistafjord was dry-docked at the Aker shipyard in Oslo for the last time. In fact, she became the last in a long line of Norwegian America liners to do so. The Sagafjord was dry-docked at the same time, but at Todd Shipyards in New York rather than at home in Norway. In the future both ships would use foreign yards for their annual overhauls. For instance, the Vistafjord visited CMR Marseille in October 1977, Blohm & Voss in Hamburg in December 1978 and Norfolk Shipbuilding & Drydock Company in Virginia in December 1979.

On 29 June 1978 the Vistafjord ran aground in the Lilliehookfjord north of Ny-Ålesund (the world's northernmost community) in Spitsbergen. She had hit an uncharted sandbank and, as the tide ebbed, it was feared the ship might start capsizing on the spot. Therefore her four powerful tender boats were lowered

The Vistafjord in the mid-1980's, showing off her rebuilt aft decks. *(FotoFlite)*

The Vistafjord in Norwegian waters in the late 1990's. Note the various top deck additions which had been made to the ship during her time with Cunard Line. (*Arnvid Brandal*)

to act as tugs, pulling the stern in the opposite direction of the developing list. After having been pulled off the sandbank by a rescue vessel, the Vistafjord proceeded to Longyearbyen where the hull was inspected by divers. Cracks in two ballast tanks were discovered, necessitating a dry-docking. She returned to Germany via Molde and Geiranger on Norway's west coast, though some ports of call also had to be cancelled. Upon her arrival in Hamburg the ship immediately went to the Blohm & Voss shipyard for repairs.

As described in the previous chapter, the Vistafjord and Sagafjord narrowly avoided being absorbed into the Royal Viking Line fleet in 1979/80. Instead a joint venture company under the name of Norwegian America Cruises (NAC) was formed, with ownership being split 50/50 between Norwegian America and Leif Høegh & Co. Høegh eventually bought the two ships outright and NAL withdrew from the passenger shipping business altogether. Although the Vistafjord was spared the kind of radical rebuilding that the Sagafjord went through, some changes were made on board during the winter of 1980/81. Among other things, the Card Room was made into a Casino.

In May 1983, however, it was announced that Leif Høegh & Co had sold the NAC ships and brand name to the Cunard Line, a subsidiary of UK-based Trafalgar House Investments, for £47 million (equivalent to $73 million). On 25 August the Vistafjord called in her home port of Oslo for the last time under Norwegian ownership and the final cruise under the NAC house flag, a Mediterranean voyage, was completed in Genoa, Italy, in October. The Vistafjord was repainted in the Cunard livery and re-registered in the Bahamas, her new call sign being C 6 Z V.

THE CUNARD YEARS

Having been handed over to the Cunard Line, the Vistafjord immediately went into drydock at Malta Shipyards in Valletta from October until December 1983. Here she was given a $7 million refit intended to increase her profitability. By placing greater emphasis on entertainment, health and fitness, Cunard hoped to attract a slightly younger clientele. The superstructure

The Caronia in Southampton, August 2003. *(John Adams)*

The Story of Saga Rose and Saga Ruby

on Promenade and Sun Decks was extended aft with a new section of seven penthouse balcony suites. A new two-deck Club Viking nightclub overlooking the stern was also added, while in the location of the original Club Viking 15 deluxe cabins were built. Forward on Main Deck some of the crew accommodation was turned into seven new passenger cabins, with another two being built in place of the Photo Shop on A Deck. In order to accommodate the increased number of passengers in a single sitting, the Vista Dining Room was extended forward by removing four passenger cabins. Some changes were made in other public areas as well. On Veranda Deck the Library/Writing Room and Casino switched locations, as did the Beauty Parlour and Barber Shop on Upper Deck. Down on C Deck, the gymnasium was modified to include a larger exercise area with the latest fitness equipment, the spa operation being entrusted to the renowned Golden Door. The Vistafjord emerged from the refit with a new passenger capacity of 695 in 389 cabins. The ship's gross tonnage had increased to 24,116 and the net tonnage to 9,356.

During her time with Cunard the Vistafjord would undergo a number of refits, usually carried out in Valletta by Malta Shipyards. In 1985 interior refurbishment work was continued both in the public areas and cabins. In addition to regular maintenance being carried out to various public rooms, the Writing Room was converted into a Computer Learning Centre featuring seven IBM workstations. At the same time, she was fitted with a new pair of four-bladed Stone Manganese propellers (with a diameter of 4.9 metres and a weight of 9.4 tons) designed to offer better fuel economy and reduce vibration, and the air conditioning plant was modernised. During a November 1990 dry-docking a new sports area was built aft of the funnel on Vistafjord's top deck, featuring two golf putting greens and shuffleboard. This area was protected by a large windshield on either side, altering the ship's exterior appearance. At the same time a new Gift Shop was built in the space of the Computer Learning Centre, which was removed. The Golden Door spa was completely refurbished, and all passenger cabins were provided with a television offering films and news channels.

In the 1980's the Vistafjord became a celebrity of sorts. A double episode of the hit TV show The Love Boat was filmed on board in May 1985 during a Norwegian fjords cruise. Later the ship was also used as the setting for a MacGyver episode. Earlier, in 1983, a movie called Table for Five had been shot on board, and during 1981/82 she had even been the star of Traumschiff (the German version of The Love Boat), six episodes of which were shot in the Caribbean.

On 10 November 1987 a valve in the engine room failed and seawater penetrated the cooling system of the six auxiliary engines, all of which subsequently shut down. The Vistafjord, which was on a 13-day Caribbean cruise from Port Everglades, Florida, was docked in Grand Cayman when this occurred. Without the air conditioning plant working, temperatures on board reached 40 degrees Celsius and many passengers spent the night out on deck. Three of the auxiliary engines were eventually restarted and the ship was able to continue her cruise, although the next port of call, in Jamaica, had to be dropped in order to get back on schedule.

In November 1994 the Vistafjord underwent a $15 million refit in Malta. Tillberg Design of Sweden was responsible for refurbishing most of the ship's public rooms, including the Ballroom, Dining Room, Garden Lounge, North Cape Bar and Pursers' Square. On the upper level of the Club Viking nightclub a new Italian-themed restaurant called Tivoli was created. 11 new suites were added, including two forward-facing duplex penthouses on the top deck. The nine other suites were built in an area of former officers' cabins on Bridge Deck, with the officers being moved to former passenger cabins on A Deck. At the same time all cabins had their bathrooms renewed. Vistafjord's gross tonnage increased to 24,492 and the displacement to 20,985 tons, while the deadweight capacity decreased to 5,867 tons. The ship now had capacity for 677 passengers in 356 cabins.

February 1997 marked the beginning of some gruelling months on board the Vistafjord. On the 11th of that

Saga Ruby in Malta in February 2005, ready to begin her new career with Saga. *(Saga)*

month, while the ship was sailing near Punta Arenas, Chile, fires broke out in a storeroom forward on D Deck and outside the laundry on C Deck. A second and more serious fire occurred in the early hours of 6 April 1997 when the Vistafjord was on her way from Florida to Malta. She was forced to alter course to Freeport in the Bahamas, where the 569 passengers were evacuated. With the remainder of her cruise cancelled, the Vistafjord sailed empty to Malta for repairs and scheduled maintenance work to be carried out. The damage to the ship was estimated at $684,845. Then, just before she was to set sail on her first post-refit cruise from Malta to the Greek islands, there was yet another fire on board. The local police department launched its own investigation into the matter and the Vistafjord was not permitted to leave her berth, the 593 passengers being sent home. All of the fires had started in crew areas and six crew members

The beautiful Saga Ruby - considered by many to be the last "classic" passenger ship ever built. *(Saga)*

were eventually dismissed. Cunard, however, took no chances with the safety of their passengers and even employed Gurkha guards on board the Vistafjord.

With the Sagafjord having already left the Cunard fleet, during the spring of 1997 the Vistafjord too was rumoured to be for sale. Neckermann Seereisen, a German tour operator, was said to be interested in acquiring her. However, despite the recent bad publicity, the Vistafjord would remain with Cunard for a few more years. Following the sale of the company from the Norwegian Kværner conglomerate to the Miami-based Carnival Corporation – the world's largest cruise ship operator – in 1998, a restructuring of the brand took place. The Cunard Line was to concentrate on promoting its ocean liner heritage, and this involved both the Queen Elizabeth 2 and the Vistafjord being treated to refits. It was decided that the former Norwegian America liner should be renamed Caronia, a name that had once graced a famous 1949-built Cunard cruise ship and, earlier, a transatlantic liner completed in 1905.

On 20 November 1999 the Vistafjord completed her final cruise in Southampton. She sailed to the Lloyd Werft yard in Bremerhaven, Germany, where she was given a $5 million refit. Some interior refurbishment under the direction of Tillberg Design took place and the hull was painted in Cunard's traditional charcoal-grey livery. On 7 December, with the name Caronia on her bow and stern, the ship sailed for Liverpool where she berthed at the Pier Head in front of the old Cunard Building. Here a formal renaming ceremony took place on 10 December, with Cunard's President and CEO Pamela Conover serving as godmother. Also present was the British Deputy Prime Minister John Prescott, himself a former Cunard employee, who announced that the Caronia would be reflagged to the United Kingdom. The ceremony ended with a fireworks display and the Caronia set her course for Southampton with invited guests on board. On 18 December she departed on her first cruise under her new name, sailing across the Atlantic to the Caribbean for the Millennium celebrations.

The transfer of the Caronia to British registry (her new call sign was M Z F P 7) meant that the ship had to comply with new stability requirements. She was out of service from 18 May until 3 June 2000, paying another visit to the Lloyd Werft yard. It had been the intention to add sponsons to her stern, but instead more permanent ballast was added in the double bottom tanks and additional water-tight doors were installed. Fortunately the Caronia's beautiful hull lines remained unspoiled.

THE SAGA YEARS

Following the successful introduction of Saga Rose in 1997, the Saga Group soon began evaluating options for the expansion of their cruise operation. In 2001 the company was reportedly close to ordering a new-build, but nothing came to pass. Saga was, however, actively keeping an eye out for a second hand ship. At about this time the Caronia was in fact offered for sale by the Carnival Corporation (Cunard's parent company). The delivery of the ship would not take place until the autumn of 2004 and in the meantime, to boost passenger capacity, Saga Pearl was chartered for the summer seasons of 2003 and 2004.

Following the completion of her final Cunard cruise on 1 November 2004, the Caronia set her course for Malta Shipyards in Valletta. It was here, on 7 November, that Saga took formal possession of the ship. The names Saga Crown and Saga Orchid had both been suggested for the Caronia, but in the end the company decided on Saga Ruby.

Quite extraordinarily for a 32-year old ship, Saga Ruby was treated to an extensive £17 million refit. The hull was sandblasted before being repainted in dark blue, during which time the name Vistafjord could be seen outlined on the stern. Alison Clixby of Clixby Associates was in charge of the interior refurbishment, which saw many areas being stripped down to their original bare steel bulkheads. Clixby had previously been responsible for refurbishment work on Saga Rose when she was working for SMC Design. In contrast to the traditional character of Saga Rose's public rooms, Saga Ruby was given a more contemporary style. The biggest changes were made aft on Veranda Deck where the Lido Restaurant was expanded and a new but smaller outdoor swimming pool was created. Compared to Saga Rose there would be an additional dining venue, the reservations-only View Restaurant, located on the upper level of the former Club Polaris. Also, a deckhouse housing a new Fitness Centre was built aft on the top deck. A water mist system was installed throughout the ship's interiors to comply with new fire safety requirements, and the machinery was given a thorough overhaul. At the same time a new Cummins KTA 3067-G type auxiliary engine with an output of 750 kW was added.

Saga Ruby was floated out of the drydock on 27 January 2005 and set sail for Southampton with outfitters still at work on board, berthing at the Mayflower Cruise Terminal on 7 February. On 25 February a formal renaming ceremony was held in the ship's Ballroom, during which Virginia Goodsell, the wife of Saga Group's Executive Chairman Andrew Goodsell, served as godmother. The ship then departed from Southampton on a two-day shakedown cruise with invited guests to Zeebrugge, Belgium.

Saga Ruby in her former home port of Oslo, July 2006.

(Anders Johannessen)

On 1 March 2005 Saga Ruby began her first cruise with fare-paying passengers, sailing from Southampton on a 32-day voyage to the Azores, the Caribbean and Bermuda. A few months later at Dover on 20 July, she met up with her former Norwegian America fleet mate for the first time in Saga colours.

The tenth anniversary of Saga Cruises fell on 2007 and on 6 and 7 March, both Saga Rose and Saga Ruby were in Sydney for a very special celebration. The Sydney Opera House held a performance of Handel's landmark opera Alcina exclusively for the ships' passengers. This black-tie event was hosted by Executive Chairman Andrew Goodsell and his wife, Virginia, and was an enormous success. The following evening, both vessels sailed against the backdrop of an enormous fireworks display, lighting up the iconic Sydney Harbour for an unforgettable experience.

On 29 May 2007 Saga Ruby arrived in North Shields on the Tyne to begin a series of cruises from Newcastle. It was the first time the ship had returned to her birthplace since being delivered from Swan Hunter as the Vistafjord 34 years earlier, and the event did not pass unnoticed. Many spectators turned out to witness Saga Ruby – the last major passenger ship built in the United Kingdom – sail up the river. Later that day the BBC came on board and a formal reception was held for local dignitaries.

A classic beauty, Saga Ruby is likely to sail on for some time under the Saga house flag as the last surviving Norwegian America liner. Already unique amongst cruise ships, with each passing year she becomes even more special – surely her equal will never again be built.

Saga Ruby in Pictures

All photos: Anders Johannessen

Lounges & restaurants

Lounges & restaurants

Lounges & restaurants

Stairs

Decks

Bridge

Parting Words

CAPTAIN DAVID WARDEN-OWEN
I well remember the day in the summer of 1997 when I first took command of Saga Rose. Not only did Rose look like a proper ship with her stylish lines, but also her indescribable aura of style and elegance was immediately evident. It is little wonder that this dame of the seas was once the pride of the Norwegian merchant fleet.

The challenges ahead were enormous but her new owner was committed to restoring Saga Rose to her former classic 5 star glory. After an extensive refit in Southampton, Saga Rose emerged looking very different in her new livery with dark blue hull and deep yellow funnel with its narrow white band and black top. Internally the new design was one that was wholly in harmony with classic style, combining her original Scandinavian elegance with décor more suited to British taste. A testimony to the commitment of the company in restoring this ship to her former, almost legendary glory, and of the dedication of her caring and highly competent crew who continue to deliver such a sincere, high level of service and attention to detail.

Eleven years ago, in 1998, I was both proud and privileged to be Master of Saga Rose on her first Saga World Cruise. The 11 years have passed by remarkably quickly and today it is with similar pride, though this time, tinged with sadness, that I am in command of Saga Rose on her final cruise. It has been a marvellous experience to navigate this historic liner to the ends of the earth and to many places in between. Her final home coming will be a very emotional time for many of us.

And so let us treasure our memories as we bid a fond farewell to Saga Rose.

"A legend in her time"

CAPTAIN ALISTAIR MCLUNDIE

Saga Rose has created a unique relationship between myself the Master, the crew, management and passengers as she has been our comfortable home for many years. We have experienced many exciting times together. She has done everything I ask of her, in any weather, and has sailed us all safely around the world. It has been the highlight of my career and a real privilege to be such an integral part of the history of this fine old lady.

HOTEL DIRECTOR HORST PINT

I have spent 18 years on board both Sagafjord and Vistafjord which are now our Saga Rose and Saga Ruby. Both ships are unique and with one departing, we shall keep Rose's memory alive in Ruby's future years to come.

Saga Rose was always my favourite, my first love so to say. She is not just a working place for me but more a place where my life was shaped , career wise and in private, how else would I have found another wonderful lady, Lyn, my wife! This grand dame was an eye catcher then as she is now and it is with a heavy heart when I say "Goodbye, the time has come to part but I shall never forget you and the hundreds of great moments you have given me, Servus und gruess gott".

HOTEL DIRECTOR EDDY DENAEGHAL

I fondly remember my time as Hotel Director on Saga Rose and even prior to it being part of the Saga fleet, when I was for many years the wine steward on the then Sagafjord.

My Martini cocktail was a big hit with the regular world cruise passengers whose only demands were that the ship would remain in Hong Kong for three days to allow the ladies to replenish their outfits at their favourite tailors. She is a special ship which will be fondly remembered and truly missed.

**CRUISE DIRECTOR
ROY PARKINSON**

When I was asked in 2000 to join Saga Shipping as Cruise Director on Saga Rose, I couldn't have been more delighted. I had worked on board previously, under her previous ownership as the Sagafjord and knew what a spacious and elegant ship she was. Under Saga ownership, all the beautiful features of Saga Rose have been lovingly maintained and enhanced, making it no surprise to anyone that she has become such a favourite with passengers and crew alike.

**LEN BLINSTON, FORMER
CHIEF ENGINEER**

When I first embarked Saga Rose as her Chief Engineer in April 1997 I immediately felt that this elegant and graceful lady would become a big part of my working life. The two major refits which followed and the next seven years prior to my move to her sister, Saga Ruby, proved to be amongst the most rewarding and happy years of my long seagoing career. Built in a bygone era of excellence in engineering and ship building craftsmanship she will be a hard act to follow. Farewell Saga Rose. "They don't build'em like you anymore..."

All photos: Saga

Original Saga Rose crew members

Former Sagafjord crew members re-unite

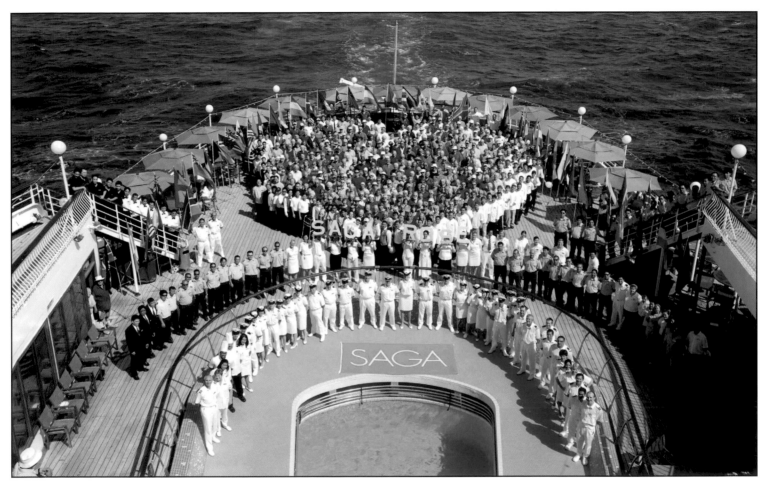

Saga Rose's officers and crew gather on the aft deck during the ship's final World Cruise. *(Saga)*

Saga Rose's Filipino choir group together with Captain David Warden-Owen. *(Saga)*

Participants in Saga Rose's first World Cruise in 1998 pictured in Gibraltar on the ship's final World Cruise in 2009.
Back row, left to right - John Williams, Derek Wigglesworth, Jimmy Hendrick, Barbara Goodyear.
Front row, left to right - Captain Warden-Owen, Brenda Wigglesworth, Alice Hendrick, Barbara Williams, Pam Collins. *(Saga)*

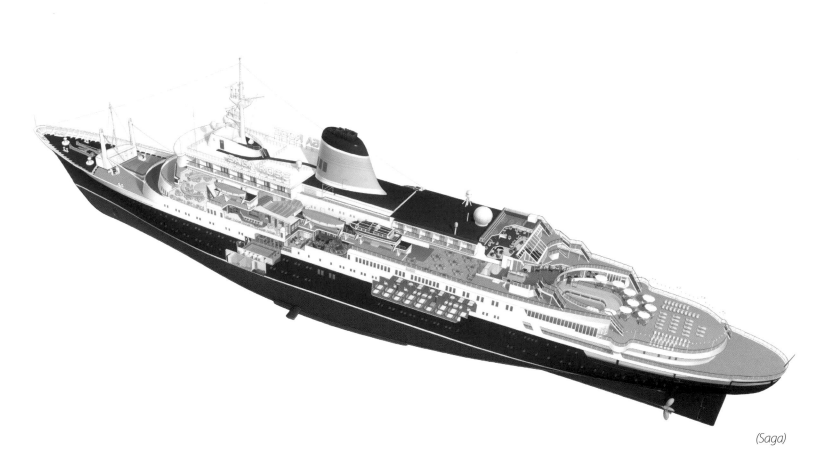

(Saga)

MV Saga Rose · **Gross tonnage:** 24,528 · **Net tonnage:** 9,110 · **Displacement:** 20,552t · **Deadweight:** 4,089t
Length overall: 188.88m (167.64m b.p.) · **Beam:** 24.38m · **Draft:** 8.33m · **Passenger capacity:** 587 · **Cabins:** 325
Crew: 352 · **Passenger decks:** 7 · **Lifts:** 4 · **Main engines:** 2 x Sulzer 9RD68 @ 12,000BHP · **Speed:** 18 knots

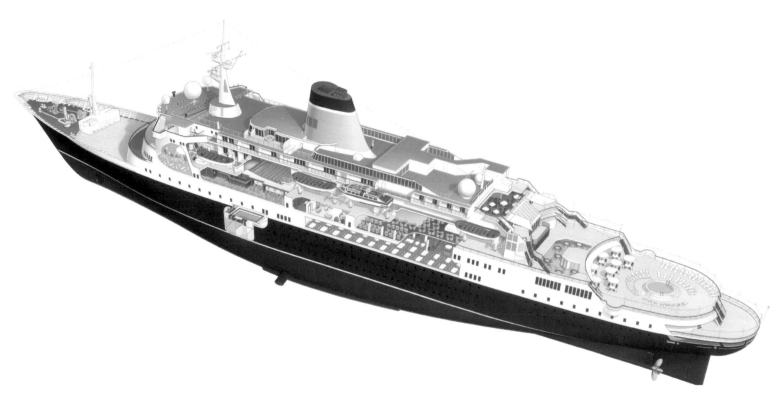

(Saga)

MV Saga Ruby · **Gross tonnage:** 24,492 · **Net tonnage:** 9,356 · **Displacement:** 20,985t · **Deadweight:** 5,867t
Length overall: 191.08m (167.64m b.p.) · **Beam:** 24.38m · **Draft:** 8.52m · **Passenger capacity:** 661 · **Cabins:** 347
Crew: 380 · **Passenger decks:** 7 · **Lifts:** 6 · **Main engines:** 2 x Sulzer 9RD68 @ 12,000BHP · **Speed:** 20 knots

Bibliography & Sources

BOOKS

Harvey, Clive and Cartwright, Roger:	*The Saga Sisters*, Tempus Publishing 2005
Hutchings, David F.:	*Caronia: Legacy of a Pretty Sister*, Shipping Books Press 2000
Kludas, Arnold:	*Vergnügungsreisen zur See: eine Geschichte der deutschen Kreuzfahrt – Band 2: 1952 bis heute*, Convent Verlag 2003 *Die grossen Passagierschiffe der Welt*, Koehlers Verlagsgesellschaft 2006
Kolltveit, Bård:	*Amerikabåtene*, The Norwegian Maritime Museum 1984
Peter, Bruce:	*Passenger Liners Scandinavian Style*, Carmania Press 2003

MAGAZINES AND PERIODICALS

Ferries - Das Fährschiffahrtsmagazin :	*"Saga Rose und Saga Ruby – zwei unzertrennliche Schwestern"* by Uwe Jacob in No. 1/2006 (pgs. 28-32) and No. 2/2006 (pgs. 25-30)
Motor Ship, The:	*"Sagafjord: French-built Flagship of Norske Amerikalinje for Cruising and Transatlantic Services"* November 1960 issue (pgs. 342-356) *"Classic lines for Norwegian America cruise ship built by Swan Hunter"* July 1973 issue (pgs. 181-186)
Shipbuilding and Shipping Record:	*"Sagafjord: The new F.C.M.-built Norwegian America Line cruise liner"* 14 October 1965 issue (pgs. 518-526) *"Swan Hunter completes cruise liner for Norwegian America Line"* 25 May 1973 issue (pgs. 19-25)

OTHER MATERIAL

Brochures, fact sheets, newsletters and press releases issued by the Norwegian America Line, Cunard Line and Saga.

ACKNOWLEDGEMENTS

Many individuals have contributed to this book in the form of information and/or illustrations. I am indebted to Bård Kolltveit and Lisa Benson at the Norwegian Maritime Museum, Michael Gallagher at Cunard Line, John Adams, Arnvid Brandal, Pam Massey, Marc Piché, Dr. Allan Ryszka-Onions, Burkhard Schütt, Ian Shiffman and Gordon Turner.

Special thanks go to Grant Laversuch, Operations Director at Saga Shipping, without whom this book would not have been published. Thanks also to Captains Philip Rentell, David Warden-Owen and Kees Spekman and Hotel Director Horst Pint. Finally I would like to thank my publishers, William and Brenda Mayes of Overview Press, and my patient and talented graphic designer Marcus Kjeldsen.

Published for Saga Shipping by
Overview Press Limited
Mayes House
Vansittart Estate
Windsor
SL4 1SE
England
www.overviewpress.co.uk

Printed by The Amadeus Press, Cleckheaton, England

Layout by Marcus Kjeldsen, www.contrafei.com

ISBN: 978-0-9547206-5-0

Saga Shipping is part of the Saga Group, proudly
serving the over 50's for more than 55 years.

Contact us at:
The Saga Building, Enbrook Park, Folkestone, CT20 3SE
www.saga.co.uk

ABOUT THE AUTHOR

Anders Johannessen (1983) has been
fascinated with passenger ships
since childhood. His keen interest
in cruise ships and ocean liners has
led him to write extensively on these
subjects. Johannessen holds a BSc in
Media and Communication Studies
from Oslo University College and
is a contributor to Cruise Business
Review, a leading trade journal.

Cover photo: *Saga*

Title page: Saga Ruby and Saga Rose in Funchal
during their 2006 World Cruises. *(Saga)*